Love and Other Small Wars
a collection of poetry

by Donna-Marie Riley

WORDS DANCE PUBLISHING
WordsDance.com

1st Edition
ISBN: 978-0615931111

Cover & Interior Design by Amanda Oaks

Words Dance Publishing
WordsDance.com

*for everyone I love
and no one in particular*

Love and Other Small Wars

Love and Other Small Wars
Donna-Marie Riley

i.

ii.

iii.

iv.

v.

i.

(*Love is an indulgence, too.*)

How to Love Your Depressed Lover

Last night I thought I kissed
the loneliness from out your belly button.
I thought I did, but later you sat up,
all bones and restless hands, and told me
there is a knot in your body that I cannot undo.

I never know what to say to these things.
"It's okay." "Come back to bed."
"Please don't go away again."

Sometimes you are gone for days at a time
and it is all I can do not to call the police,
file a missing person's report, even though
you are right there, still sleeping next to me
in bed. But your eyes are like an empty house
in winter: lights left on to scare away intruders.

Except in this case I am the intruder and you
are already locked up so tight that no one
could possibly jimmy their way in.

Last night I thought I gave you a reason
not to be so sad when I held your body like
a high note and we both trembled from the effort.

Some people, though, are sad against all reason,
all sensibility, all love. I know better now.
I know what to say to the things you admit to me
in the dark, all bones and restless hands.

"It's okay." "You can stay in bed."
"Please come back to me again."

Consequences

My brother holds his boyfriend's hand
the way you might hold a loaded gun.

The first time they kissed,
he came home and apologized to me,
said he was sorry for all the nights
I'd found him bending himself into origami,
said he thought if he folded in enough edges,
he might escape what he really was.

He asked me not to tell our parents,
begged until he was blue in the face
with his fear.

They found out by accident,
caught them fondling each other
in the back yard, told him,
"how could we be disappointed
in your ability to love so hands on?"

My brother thought this was the end,
thought with their acceptance he would
no longer have need to hide himself
like a dirty magazine, thought
he'd finally found freedom.

Three weeks after this incident,
my brother sat in ICU for nine days
without sleep.

A mob of kids,
disgusted by two men kissing,
worked their fists into
his boyfriend like dough,
beat him tender, left him for dead.

His boyfriend recovered from the
injuries, but not from the insult.

He began to twitch at shadows,
refused to see movies past 8 PM,
would only kiss my brother in either
of their bedrooms, provided
the blinds were drawn shut.

The first time they made love,
my brother came to me afterwards with
an ache in his eyes and choke in his voice,
told me they'd burned their bodies up
like matches and were now afraid
of who might smell the smoke.

The Battle I've Made of Loving Me

Zelda Fitzgerald once wrote to Scott, *"I'm sorry for
all the times I've been mean and hateful."*

I wonder why we throw our weight at the ones we love
instead of our kisses. I wonder why we learn to be quiet
instead of kind. I know my silence is the reason
you talk in your sleep, say things like *how can you love me*
over and over until I ask myself the same thing in your voice.

Do you remember the time I wanted to be a kite so I threw
myself off the cliff by your mother's house thinking the wind
would catch me? When they asked me in the hospital why
I'd done it, I told them I had meant to fly and that it was
a surprise to me when I had fallen like an anvil. I didn't know
my heart was that heavy. I didn't know it was a bag of rocks.

The truth is: I think I use you as a punching bag for all the
fight inside me. I've made a soldier of your eyes for
all the things they've had to witness. I am sorry for the bags
underneath them that I have packed with so much luggage.

Maybe we say to those that love us the things we know
no one else would forgive us for. So *I am sorry for all the
times I've been mean and hateful.* I'm sorry for the cliff.
I'm sorry for the war I have made of my body and how it
is one you'll never win. I'm sorry for the silence.

I'm sorry my heart is heavy and that I use it as a weapon.
I'm sorry it is the reason you talk in your sleep, say things
like *is it always going to be this hard?* I'm sorry that it is.

Advice for Anyone Wise Enough to Listen

When the girl with the ceramic voice
and the tags cut out of her nightgowns
asks you to stay the night, *stay*.

She needs it.

Don't take her body heat for granted.
Don't interpret it as an invitation.
She is not an open house. She is not for sale.

She is wet asphalt and strange hands
pressed into it. She is cough syrup and booze,
cigarettes and *I bet your mother warned you
about girls like me.*

When she reaches for your hand in her sleep,
let her have it. She is looking for an anchor.
She is looking for anything sturdy enough to
keep her here.

Be her little piece of faith.
Give her something to believe in.

Remind her people can be good.
Remind her people can be trusted.
Remind her that she *is* beautiful.

In the morning, she will be silent and scared.
She will not make you coffee. She will not
make you at home. She will show you to the
door and lock it behind you.

Do not be alarmed by this.
Do not forget her name. Do not refuse
to leave as if she owes you something.
You are not a debt she has to pay off.

When a girl asks you to stay the night,

she is really asking you to love her.

So love her.

Love her quiet. Love her gentle.
Love her like she is made
of daisy petals and talcum powder.

She is.

Go Gently About Your Love

There are days you are impossible
to comfort. The days I find you kissing
your knees, I know to distance myself
from you however much it turns
my heart to orange pulp.

On these days, I use my indoor voice.
I draw you baths of lavender,
leave you letters in the steam of mirrors,
tell anyone who calls that you are sleeping.

You don't say a word all night,
but you look at me with eyes full of
apology, eyes like flickering street lamps
that are sorry to be restless.

Darling, I have watched you become
lonely all at once, watched your smile
go slick like oil, your shoulders sag
as beds will when they have been
loved in for too many years.

Nothing soothes you.

I have tried the incense sticks,
the Chamomile lotion,
the jasmine tea, the silence.

There is nothing to be done for you.
I am ready to forgive myself for that.

I am ready to stop viewing your
sadness as a failing on my part.

All I can do is wait for your hand
to seek mine in the dark when
we both think the other is sleeping.

The Heart of the Matter

Let's tell the truth about the way we love each other. Let's display our bloody hands palms up, let the hunger in our bellies tell of our well-disguised violence. We never loved each other lightly. No, we never took the ballet classes our mothers signed us up for as children. We crushed beetles into dust, pulled grass up from its roots laughing. We showed too much teeth. We had voices of gravel, knees like skinned peaches. We signed letters under names that were not ours, forced people into forgetting us. You and I liked to set things on fire only to put them out again. Still do (think of your loins, think of my temper). Our fathers gave us BB guns instead of Barbie dolls. We shot down birds to examine their wings, buried them in old Metallica t-shirts and laundry detergent boxes. We love each other like that. We love each other limp; love each other 'til the water runs clear; love each other like a good, clean shot.

ii.
(Sometimes the fight is small,
but the struggle is big.)

Exhibit X

I learned in school that war is what happens
when nations disagree, but the textbooks never told me
that war is also what happens when parents disagree,
and when children throw insults harder than they hit baseballs
and when I cannot force myself out of bed in the morning
because there is a voice in my head that tells me
I might win the battle, but I will not win the –

War is what happens when teachers call on students
who don't have the answers and they are left
fighting their father once he sees their report card.
War is what happens when it rains so hard
blades of grass bend over defeated.
War is what happens over telephone wires when a son
tells his mother he is gay and her white flag
of surrender is the phone going dead.

I have seen war burst into being the moment girls think
they're too old to hold hands and again some years later when
they're too young to do more than that, but charge forward regardless
only to end up with semen exploding inside them like shrapnel.

I have seen war across some people's wrists.
I have seen it in bones trying to revolt from the flesh.
I have seen it in eyes like double whiskey shots
that are drunk off self-hatred.

I was taught that war was loud. It was supposed to be
bombs and a dictator's speech and the sound of an entire race
being crossed off one by one, like the days of a calendar.
And I can agree that this is war, but war can also be quiet.

It can be as quiet as a miscarriage.
Or the therapy sessions afterwards, which is quieter even.

It can be as silent as a gas leak.

They asked me in sixth grade what war meant to me

and I told them about the Holocaust, I told them about the Jews.
I didn't tell them about the boy across the road from me
whose father used his forearms as ashtrays and whose eyes
were the American flag: star-spangled.

I didn't tell them about women that have their bodies claimed
like new worlds, or men who punch walls and wear their bruised knuckles
like honor badges for all the tears they haven't cried because
they were raised to be soldiers and soldiers do not cry.

I didn't mention any of these things because I was taught
that war was big. It was something that happened between countries
and it happened with armies and guns and nuclear weapons.

But if they asked me now—if they asked me now
what war meant to me, I would tell them that war is what happens
inside people, and I would show them this poem as my evidence.

My

After Jeanann Verlee

My need. My blue hands.
My should–have–knocked. My worry.
My too many phone calls. My selfish.
My *don't stop.* My *it's okay.*
My cold feet. My steal your sweater.
My keep the lights on. My *keep going.*
My nervous. My bitten lips.
My soft body. My hard words.
My *try harder.* My *try harder.*
My try. My give up.
My hug the knees. My want.
My talking to strangers. My talking
to no one. My talking to myself.
My no sense of direction.
My *touch me, don't touch me!*
My cool eyes. My quick temper.
My *I don't know what's wrong.*
My *I trust you, but where are you going?*
My *I trust you, but who's on the phone?*
My *I trust you.* My lies come easy.
My naked photos.
My body an open wound.
My body an open fist.
My *come back later.* My *hold me.*
My please. My please. My *please.*
My *fuck you.* My *leave me.*
My *why don't you leave me?*
My *it hurts.* My heart of coral.
My *no.* My *now.* My *marry me.*
My *why don't you want to marry me?*
My bad days. My bad weeks.
My bad. My *I'm sorry, but—*
My *told-you-so.* My scold.
My *it still hurts.* My bad dreams.
My run. My come back.
My *take me back.* My *take me home.*
My *take me, take me, take me.*

My quiet beg. My loose lips.
My *let go.* My call-it-quits.
My *call your mother.*
My double standards. My jealous.
My *explain yourself.* My *shh.*
My headaches. My bent spine.
My *stay home.* My *stay.*
My go. My going.
My gone too long.
My come back. Again.
My come back.

How to Be Alone: A Twelve-Step Program

1.
Forget about his hands.
Yes, they are beautiful.
Yes, they are large and strong
and full of callus.

Yes, they made mincemeat
out of you.

2.
Put your bitterness away.
You have carried it around so long
your eyes have turned to brine.

3.
When he tries to welcome himself
into your new apartment, lock the door.

When he tries to welcome himself
into your liquor cabinet, send him home.

When he tries to welcome himself
into your body, call the police.

Tell them this is not his first offense.

4.
Call your mother.
She coughs and sputters and
talks over you. Call her anyway.

Use the telephone connection
like an umbilical cord.

Remember that you are the

only person who knows what her
heart sounds like from the inside.

5.
Go outside.
Eat a picnic of mango
and Dr Pepper.

Allow the heat to melt your
hardness into jelly.

6.
When the shy boy from Apartment B
asks you out to dinner, say yes.

Order anything but salad.

Kiss him goodnight.

Say thank you.

7.
Read the books on the living room
shelf. And the ones in the closet.
And the ones under your bed.

Lose yourself in things other than
a stranger's mouth.

8.
Adopt a cat.

9.
When your friends complain
that you are anti-social,

draw the blinds, put your phone
on silent, cocoon yourself in
blankets and drink hot chocolate.

Enjoy every minute of it.

10.
Leave time for being productive.

11.
Learn to love yourself
like it is the hardest math equation
you have ever been asked to solve.

12.
Learn to love yourself like
no one will ever do it any better.

No one will.

A Conversation with My Grief, Which I Have Nick-Named Margaret
After Desireé Dallagiacomo

I avoid the word,
tip-toe around the implications,
laugh like I mean it, like it doesn't hurt,
like my throat isn't full of nettles,
like my body has never had to brace itself
against knuckles rolled inside a doughy fist.
They got me, Margaret. They were always
going to. Now I have eyes narrowed
into back road alleyways.
Now my tongue has turned to salt
in my mouth. Now my voice
loses itself in every fight.
The self-help books say: *forgive.*
The antidepressants say: *forget.*
My body says: *take blame.*
I blame it for being soft.
I blame the gap between my thighs,
blame my breasts, blame my smile.
Blame myself.
I blame myself, Margaret.
I did it. I opened like the mouth of
a river. I twisted into pretzel knots.
I have dirty knees, Margaret.
I have dirtier stories.
I am dirty, Margaret.
I couldn't stop the blood.
Couldn't fight back.
I was the fat to all of their muscle.
And I have a heart, Margaret.
I had a heart. But I have minced it
between my ribs. I have heaved
the rest into the toilet bowl.
I have fed it sleeping pills and shame.
I don't trust it, Margaret. Don't want
to feel it red and sweet, a cherry ready
to burst between someone's teeth.

I don't want to feel, Margaret.
I sleep until noon, barely eat,
watch as my body shrinks in
upon itself. Wait for the bones
to show cleanly through the flesh.
The doctor says:
eat well, exercise, love yourself.
The suicide hotline says:
don't be selfish.
My body says: *disappear.*
My body is convinced
it is a threat to itself.
My body is hollowed out
like a Halloween pumpkin.
It's a gimmick, Margaret. All of this.
This is all a ploy to get us to feel
guilty for our own attraction.
For our lack thereof.
For our ugliness, our hardness,
our pliable limbs, our heaviness,
our audacity to say *no.*
The media says:
victim-blaming, slut-shaming.
The statistics say:
One in every five women.
My body finally stands up
and says: *I am not at fault here.*
My body is retracting its apologies.
There's nothing to forgive, Margaret.
My body is not a regret.

A Toast

Here's to the boy with the impeccable jaw line and the neat mouth. Here's to his few scars and his frequent silence. Here's to all the chances you insist on giving him, regardless of whether he asks for them. Here's to how he sleeps soundly through your crying. Here's to the empty space he has created inside you, but refuses to fill. Here's to how his collared-shirts fit lovingly around his wrists. Here's to his wandering eye. Here's to his lack of apologies. Here's to his late nights and your abandoned body. Here's to his hand slipping inside you without invitation. Here's to his laughing about it later. Here's to his logic; the constant rationalizing of every wondrous thing that makes you curious. Here's to the crooks of his elbows. Here's to his softer features, the ones you write into all your characters. Here's to his quiet indifference. Here's to always coming out looking worse. Here's to your sadness being folded up and put away with all your laundry. Here's to his blank stare. To his false smile. To his rather-be-doing-something-else. Here's to his let go. To his no fight. To his clean knuckles. Here's to all of this. And none of it. Here's to you deserve more.

for Jeanann Verlee

She writes as if she is full of stone
and a silence that won't sit still any longer.

I wonder how long she has pushed stories
into the cavities of her teeth. After a while,
the secrets we keep start to keep us.

She has a sweet voice until she reads,
a voice of elderflower and honey drizzle.

It is the poems that turn it to scratch.
The poems turn it to salt, turn it to hiss.
Turn to God, they say.

He will love you like a Sunday.
He will love you gentle.
Love you like prayer.

This woman does not need to be loved
like prayer. This woman needs to be loved
like a fist that won't strike, like a mouth
full of spit, like *life*, like *real*.

Or else she has had too much of that already.
Or else she has arms like scratch cards,
eyes of flint, a tongue curled up like the ears
of a dog that has been kicked too much
and had it called love.

Or else she doesn't want it at all.
She wants to keep her body like a secret,
wrap it up in silk, in velvet. Who can blame her?

When her body has been used like quicksand.
When her heart has been nailed to bed staffs.
When she has scars she cannot explain.

Who can blame her for her voice like a blizzard,

her voice like a machete that will cut you in two?

Who can blame her for the stones in her body
that make her footfalls heavy where lovers
demand they be light?

A woman like this has no business being light.

Light women are blown off course by gusts
of wind that barely push. A woman like her,
a woman full of stone, she has taken one
blow after another and she is still here.

She is still tall. She wears her spine like
a war medal. She has come home safely,
but she is still prepared to fight.

iii.

(All of our stories come first from blood.)

*In my experience,
"family" is a word we use
against our better judgement.*

History

My mother tells me a story
about her father's fist, how it
swung like a broken porch light
into the darkness of her face.

I ask if this is her definition
of war.

Instead of answering,
she shows me a picture
of her own mother,
who fought

alongside her
and lost.

When You Have to Bury Your Father

Let the anger go.

When your sister shows you the
scar you gave her in a particularly
bad fight nineteen years ago.
When you remember the way you
hid your body like a stained cushion.
When there is blood from
the men with too much fist.

Let the anger go.
What you don't feed can't grow.
Let it wilt. Let the anger drift
like petals to the soil.

Before you lose your voice.
Before you shoot the messenger.
Before your daughter learns to shout back.

Let the anger go.
Drop it like a hot plate.
Leave it like a small town.

After the doctor diagnoses
high blood pressure. After the family
splits like orange segments. After the
ex-husband marries his new wife.

Let the anger go.
Pull it up like an anchor that has
had you stuck. Release it like a
held breath. Lose it like extra weight.

When the phone stops ringing.
When eye contact becomes too difficult.
When the letters go unanswered.

When the tears come fast.

When the years burn up.

When you have to bury your father,
let the anger go. Make peace.

Forgive.

Miscarriage

My sister has a mouth full of bleed.
She has two hazard sign eyes and a
stomach like a sieve.

In it she entrusted one child,
one tiny infant with cherry tomato toes
and spider-silk eyelashes.

When her stomach gave in,
when her stomach emptied like
a water basin, my sister got a rosary
bead tattoo and took up smoking.

If you ask her how she's doing,
she answers from a distance. Her words
are summoned from the edge of the Sahara.
Her voice rasps from all the cigarettes.

Two summers ago I found a collection
of her suicide notes stashed around the house.
I worried so much my hair turned gray.

Upon closer inspection, I realized that
each one of those notes read less like a goodbye
and more like a promise to meet that child
somewhere she trusted more than her own body.

A Poem for the Insomniacs

My mother kept me on her right hip,
sleepy-eyed and half the weight of a sigh.
She swayed like a sinking ship.

It's nearly a year now
since I last saw her. Her name
leaves my mouth in a solitary march.

I salute it out of habit.

I am old enough now to rock myself to sleep.
I do it thinking of airplanes falling from the sky
like leaves and how matches only live
for twelve seconds at most.

The first time I had trouble sleeping
I used Heineken and a hot water bottle.
The second time I peeled my legs apart like
orange slices and invited strangers in.
The third I remember losing blood.

What is the secret to a good night's sleep?

It is a mother moving her feet like a poem
while she wears you around her waist like a belt.

Lessons

In earlier years my sister had hands
stained with her own blood.
She warned me womanhood
is something that comes hot
and painful
between the legs,
whether it is just arriving,
or whether it's being taken from you.

iv.
(*I've only ever known how to give myself in two ways:
in writing and in body heat.*)

Bed

This is our sacred ground.
This is our mosque, our church, our temple,
whatever you want to call it. This is our place
of prayer. Of savior. I lay you down in linen
sheets and kiss you until you tremble,
kiss you until you shake like a hundred voices
chanting the same psalm in a wooden room.

Here is the place we lose ourselves.
Here is your body like a rowboat and mine
like a sea that will destroy it. Here is where
I give up the façade of being an innocent girl
when you touch me full of bloodlust and I open
like a flower. Here is where I hand my body over,
not like it's holy, but like it's cursed and you
are the only one who can exorcise
the screaming things out of it.

The first night we went to bed together,
I learned your body was a secret.
And an earthquake. And a promise.
And every last wish I'd ever made on
birthday candles, all neatly rolled into the
glory that is the way your hips
softly melt into the source of life itself.

The first night we made love,
I learned God exists.

I found Him in the lining of your skin.
I found Him in your throat.

How We Got Here

i.

I asked you for letters,
told you I couldn't survive off small talk.
Told you even your laughter had begun to fail me.

When it came, your handwriting resembled
nothing but a straight line held taut against
the screen of a life support machine.

ii.

You made me leave the wild parts of myself
at the front door when I visited.
They got scuffed up with the shoes.
When I wore them home, the rain got through.

iii.

The sex got too frantic,
like each of us kept trying to push
more than our bodies inside one another.
Like our fingers were constantly gripping
the edge of a cliff.

Like love could be redeemed with sweat.

iv.

When the sadness rose in me like bile,
you left the room to avoid the smell.

v.

Your ribs started to look like an escape ladder.
My mouth kept falling down the rungs.

vi.

Everything became hard work.
Our muscles burned and went out as matches.

vii.

I began to feel unwelcome in your hands.

Theories

You are wisdom. Silver-tongued and sharp. Brain the size of a small country. I theorize in bed. All speculation. All questions and no answers. You are certain. You are fact and precision and *well, obviously...* I am all blood without you. Heart. Blood and wonder and still more blood. I am infinitely curious. If it weren't for you, there'd be no conclusions to any of my conversations. Just wide, black holes. The earth opened in one giant yawn. History blurred into a question mark. Thank you for the opposition. For your tongue lying in wait. Your knowledge unsheathed and sunk deep into my softness. My far-fetched *maybes*. My asking. You say knowing is better when it can be tied up neatly. When it can be finished up and closed off. When the discussion is over. I prefer to wonder. Prefer my own imagination. Prefer ignorance. Prefer to challenge all your certainties. Your clean mouth. Boxed mind. Straight shooter you are. You solid rock. Bold, dense, and unmoving. You are a force to be reckoned with. So am I. The ocean crumbles boulders into nothing after only a few good touches.

She

She is made of coffee cream.
Of half-sunken lily pads.
Of fishtails. Of wet feathers.
She is made of fox blood.
Of exit signs.
Of shark teeth and hunger.
Of paper cuts and lemon juice.
She is made of Coca Cola.
Concentrated sugar.
Parch in the throat.
Inconceivable thirst.
She is made of cinnamon.
Candied apple and sweet tooth.
Small hands.
An elephant's memory.
She is made of split hair
and hand-me-downs.
Books fat with raindrops.
Library fines. Bus tickets.
Broken-winged sparrows.
She is made of *go*.
Of leaving, but never left.
Of long strides. Of had enough.
Of unsigned postcards.
She is made of poetry.
Of clichés. Of smudged ink
and escapism. She is made
of everything your mother
warned you about
at the dinner table:
ripped stockings,
no respect, loose morals,
asking for it.
She is made of mystery.
Coattails and cigarettes.
Whiskey shots. Cemeteries.
Made of trying too hard,
but still you love her.

Still your heart catches
in your throat when you
touch her. She is made of
tumble-dried bed sheets.
Scatter cushions.
Velvet.
She is made of dandelion spores.
Of grass blades and razor blades.
Of fear. Of bitten lips.
Stephen King novels.
Made of thunderstorms.
Of roar. Of high tide and the
entire spectrum of the color blue.
She is made of your hands:
of small courage, of violent need,
of *take*, of please, of desperate.
She is made of *your* hands,
which is to say
she is shaking.

Paris

I went to Paris,
ate the crêpes,
dined where Hemingway once sat,
stood in front of the Notre Dame,
hated, quite passionately, the lot of it.
Had to bite back on my boredom.
The Eiffel Tower is nothing but
a metal monster with an empty belly.
Its visitors smile their jaws sore,
finger cameras hung about their necks
the way a nun might do her rosary.
In the bookshop where it is rumored
Ezra Pound played James Joyce at chess,
and often lost, I scatter little notes
on the backs of receipts:
"It's all smoke and mirrors, stranger."
The River Seine is ugly
in the way everything is ugly
once you have anticipated it too long.
I did not find my faith in the Sacré Coeur,
but I did find my reason for its absence:
how God has been turned into
a tourist attraction,
no better than the rest of it.
How we will buy into anything
we are told might save us.
How we reach out blindly
for enlightenment,
often pushing others aside as we go.
There is only so long I can stand
to look in silence at a series of buildings,
all made of more or less the same thing:
brick, marble, alabaster.
I am not interested in this kind
of architecture, find more beauty
in a lover's skeleton,
built meticulously bone by bone,
plastered with flesh,
held together with blood.

*Stop loving people
into corners.*

V.
*(I am a child of January,
and of midnight, and of velvet.)*

*The closest I've come to accepting myself
is writing in a bathroom stall,
"I am not the pretty one."*

Lunar Cycle
After Catherine Pierce

At eighteen, I was quiet and impulsive,
my eyes a bonfire, my hair self-cut and uneven.
I threw my tongue like a fishing reel down the throats
of strangers, reeled their secrets up from the depths
of stomachs that echoed the way empty rooms do.

I was a Buddhist; I was Ghandi;
I was a moment of silence for all the lives we had lost.

I was insecure and in heat. I had crossed legs
and weak ankles. I took my baby teeth to a river
and skipped them over the surface. I lost my breath
in someone else's mouth. I was magnificent.

Now I look back as though through a thick heat,
as though that girl with a bitten lip and a furious walk
was nothing but a mirage I fevered myself into.

I remember her by her sadness, her sadness and her smile.
She wears the latter like a boomerang that has only now
returned home. I want to tell her instead to consider it
a half crescent moon. Consider that it will wax and wane
in that same way. We all have days when we don't feel whole.

Backseat Lover

I am a backseat lover.
My hair never smells of anything
but hot car. I keep my heart rolled down
like windows in late August;
I am hoping the wind will air it out.

Passengers get too comfortable in me.
They begin to take liberties,
flicking between radio stations,
taking full advantage of the ashtray.

They are reckless, barely avoiding
impact with trees or lamp-posts
or limping pedestrians.

I have been unhooked, unzipped, and
unabashed, lounging across three seats,
smoking cigarettes and cursing God,
cursing mouths that are only good for kissing.

Nudity does not scare me. I am aware of my
breasts and my hips and my erogenous zones.

I am aware of the consequence of hands that
touch me as if I am indented with Braille.
I am aware of entry and exit and eroticism.

I am even aware that some may fail to respond
to STOP signs. I still don't wear a seatbelt.

I sprawl out like a heat wave and I open
like a full moon. I am a backseat lover.
I don't watch the road; I enjoy the ride.

Sylvia

Sometimes I can understand
why Sylvia Plath put her head
in an oven; there are things
in my head, too,
that I would like to catch fire.

Dust to Dust

I am a campfire inside.
I am smoking.

Miles over, on the next site,
strangers point to my smoke
signals and debate the
seriousness of the matter.

I am asking for help.
I am full of please.
I am dirty mouth and
sucker punch.

They taught me to be a secret.
Keep your head down.
Keep your fists tight.
Speak as if you have a bellyache.

I'm a bellyache.
I am stomach acid.
I am a void to be filled.

Let them fill you, they said.
Let them have you.

Don't flinch. Don't cry.
Don't keep yourself locked up
like a trophy cabinet.

You are not a trophy, they said.
You are not first place.
You are not gold. You are not silver.

You are beautiful purple and indigo.
Blueberry and plum. Black eye
and track marks. You are weak.

I am weak.

I am helpless.
I am a wet cat scratching
at the back door.

I have my mother's eyes.
I have her hair and her soft
and her worry.

I am worry.
I am *is she coming home tonight*.
I am a missing person's file.

I am not coming home.
I am campfire.
I am burning.

I am ash
and I am good at it.

Amidst the Fight

You wonder how you got here.
How, after a series of rogue punches
and loose teeth, you find yourself
still with blood in your cheeks.
Find yourself still alive enough
to smile at strangers. At your mother.
At the stray dog with the mean growl.
You remember the same growl
rising in your own throat.
Remember the anger. The spit.
The heavy scent of your own breath.
Remember the urge, always, to run.
The shame in your skinny legs,
in your all-fat-no-muscle, in your
not enough, not nearly enough.
The nights you gave your body away
because giving it away was easier
than admitting it was yours,
was easier than saying no,
on those nights:
how close did you feel to the moon?
All that waning, all that
losing yourself little by little,
only to find the absent pieces
returned to you once more.
Only to find yourself whole
and white and clean again.
How, after all the self-hatred,
after the cigarette burns,
the razorblades; the sleeping pills,
the thimbles of bleach,
how you still are a
mausoleum of bones.
How the flesh stretches
over all the gained weight,
the benign cysts, the sadness.
How there is more to you than
the things you have taught your

mouth to do in the dark.
There is more to you than
bitten fingernails and
averted eye contact,
the guilt you know like
it's your own last name.
You wonder how you got here,
after all this. All this doubt.
All these hand-crafted mistakes.
All that desire to cut and run.
To leave yourself behind.
You wonder how,
amidst all this fight and knuckle
and bruise, you somehow
learned to forgive yourself.

Donna-Marie Riley is, first and foremost, a poet, albeit one with a shaking voice. At seven years old her second grade teacher personally bought her a journal and instructed her to "write everything." So she did.

The first poem she wrote without the help of her mother was entitled Leprechauns and was, quite frankly, rather terrible. Since then, however, she's worked hard at the craft, dedicating more time to it than anything (and any*one*) else. She can't say herself whether it's paid off, but she's amassed a humble following within the online Tumblr community, which helps to keep her at it even on the bad days.

She lives between homes in England, but often misses the sharp edges of New York City where she was raised. She collects old books, strange necklaces, and soft lovers. She gets nervous leaving the house without an umbrella and has trouble with the word *gone*.

Love and Other Small Wars is her first collection of poetry. She hopes you'll handle it gently.

a poem by kris ryan

Unrequited love? We've all been there.

Enter:

WHAT TO DO AFTER SHE SAYS NO
by Kris Ryan.

This skillfully designed 10-part poem explores what it's like to ache for someone. This is the book you buy yourself or a friend when you are going through a breakup or a one-sided crush, it's the perfect balance between aha, humor & heartbreak.

WHAT TO DO AFTER SHE SAYS NO
A Poem by Kris Ryan

$10 | 104 pages | 5" x 8" | softcover | ISBN: 978-0615870045

"*What to Do After She Says No* takes us from Shanghai to the interior of a refrigerator, but mostly dwells inside the injured human heart, exploring the aftermath of emotional betrayal. This poem is a compact blast of brutality, with such instructions as "Climb onto the roof and jump off. If you break your leg, you are awake. If you land without injury, pinch and twist at your arm until you wake up." Ryan's use of the imperative often leads us to a reality where pain is the only outcome, but this piece is not without tenderness, and certainly not without play, with sounds and images ricocheting off each other throughout. Anticipate the poetry you wish you knew about during your last bad breakup; this poem offers a first "foothold to climb out" from that universal experience."

— **LISA MANGINI**

"Reading Kris Ryan's *What To Do After She Says No* is like watching your heart pound outside of your chest. Both an unsettling visual experience and a hurricane of sadness and rebirth—this book demands more than just your attention, it takes a little bit of your soul, and in the end, makes everything feel whole again."

— **JOHN DORSEY**
author of **Tombstone Factory**

"*What to Do After She Says No* is exquisite. Truly, perfectly exquisite. It pulls you in on a familiar and wild ride of a heart blown open and a mind twisting in an effort to figure it all out. It's raw and vibrant...and in the same breath comforting. I want to crawl inside this book and live in a world where heartache is expressed so magnificently.

— **JO ANNA ROTHMAN**
MA, Coach & Conjurer of Electric Creative Wholeness

Tammy Foster Brewer is the type of poet who makes me wish I could write poetry instead of novels. From motherhood to love to work, Tammy's poems highlight the extraordinary in the ordinary and leave the reader wondering how he did not notice what was underneath all along. I first heard Tammy read 'The Problem is with Semantics' months ago, and it's stayed with me ever since. Now that I've read the entire collection, I only hope I can make room to keep every one of her poems in my heart and mind tomorrow and beyond.

— **NICOLE ROSS**, author

NO GLASS ALLOWED
Poetry by Tammy Foster Brewer

$12 | 56 pages | 6" x 9" | softcover | ISBN: 978-0615870007

Brewer's collection is filled with uncanny details that readers will wear like the accessories of womanhood. Fishing the Chattahoochee, sideways trees, pollen on a car, white dresses and breast milk, and so much more -- all parts of a deeply intellectual pondering of what is often painful and human regarding the other halves of mothers and daughters, husbands and wives, lovers and lost lovers, children and parents.

— **NICHOLAS BELARDES**
author of *Songs of the Glue Machines*

Tammy deftly juxtaposes distinct imagery with stories that seem to collide in her brilliant poetic mind. Stories of transmissions and trees and the words we utter, or don't. Of floods and forgiveness, conversations and car lanes, bread and beginnings, awe and expectations, desire and leaps of faith that leave one breathless, and renewed.

"When I say I am a poet / I mean my house has many windows" has to be one of the best descriptions of what it's like to be a contemporary female poet who not only holds down a day job and raises a family, but whose mind and heart regularly file away fleeting images and ideas that might later be woven into something permanent, and perhaps even beautiful. This ability is not easily acquired. It takes effort, and time, and the type of determination only some writers, like Tammy, possess and are willing to actively exercise.

— **KAREN DEGROOT CARTER**
author of *One Sister's Song*

WORDS DANCE PUBLISHING has one aim:

To spread mind-blowing / heart-opening poetry.

Words Dance artfully & carefully wrangles words that were born to dance wildly in the heart-mind matrix. Rich, edgy, raw, emotionally-charged energy balled up & waiting to whip your eyes wild; we rally together words that were written to make your heart go boom right before they slay your mind. You dig?

Words Dance Publishing is an independent press out of Pennsylvania. We work closely & collaboratively with all of our writers to ensure that their words continue to breathe in a sound & stunning home. Most importantly though, we leave the windows in these homes unlocked so you, the reader, can crawl in & throw one fuck of a house party.

To learn more about our books, authors, events & Words Dance Poetry Magazine, visit:

WORDSDANCE.COM

Made in the USA
Lexington, KY
25 October 2014